PRAISE FOR BETSY L. JORDAN

"Being Betsy's client changed my outlook on life. There are self-help books, motivational movies, thoughtful quotes that give you a 'hmmm' moment, but there's nothing like the direct dynamic impact of Betsy's approach. There is such a thing as a mental shift, or altering your mind-set. I know this now, because Betsy Jordan helped me accomplish quite a shift with her unique coaching methods. Thank you Betsy for making all the difference in my world, I have a much better grasp on business and financial responsibility than ever before."

—Daniel Jones

"Betsy, brings a great energy and enthusiasm to her work. Creative, concise and fun to work with."

—Joseph C. D'Alessandro
Independent Media Production Professional

"I hired Betsy for executive coaching, and it was one of the best decisions I've made in a while. She revitalized key aspects of my career with her thoughtful and disciplined methodology. She is so intelligent and empathetic, yet she'll tell you when your full of sh*t when you need to hear it. I highly recommend her to turbo-charge your life."

—Chip Venters

CEO at BrowsePlay Interactive Video

"Betsy is an inspired leader with energy and passion to share her many gifts and talents. I recommend her without reservation."

—Denise Cline

Member at Law Offices of Denise Smith Cline, PLLC

"Betsy exemplifies the word *transformation* for that is what she offers all of her clients. Coaching with Betsy offers direct feedback and direct results!"

—Laura Gould

Owner/Coach at SwimLessonsRaleigh.com

"On a personal level, Betsy practices what she preaches. She never stops growing and learning."

—Will

"North Carolina's film industry was well served through Betsy's insight, hard work and commitment. Betsy championed projects that promoted the industry and was able to focus on the key issues that made a difference in how North Carolina competed against other states. She's a great ally to have on your team."

—Monty Hagler
President & CEO, RLF Communications

"Betsy Jordan is a visionary who can see beyond the routine tasks of the day. She has a gift for marketing and putting together resources to accomplish her goals. Betsy is a leader and can influence others with her keen insight, clear communication style and engaging personality."

—Bob Jamieson
Living Seaside Realty Group

"I was well served through Betsy's insight, hard work and commitment. She's a great ally to have on your team."

—Monty Hagler

"Betsy is a results oriented person, one you will be glad to have had the pleasure to meet, and delighted she's always working in your best interests."

—Carol Spiller, CMB

"Betsy Jordan has a keen insight into helping people achieve their life goals. She has an uncanny knack for breaking down barriers that may be creating obstacles for people that they cannot see for themselves: a frequent life-staller; spending time with Betsy is like drinking from a cold fountain on an incredibly hot day; you always want to come back for more! Take making a change in your life seriously and give Betsy a call; you won't be sorry!"

—Anna Watson Blair

Infusion Therapy Nurse at UNC-Hospitals

"Betsy is bright and highly intuitive. Her assistance with me at a critical point in my life's journey was instrumental in helping me in many areas, both professional and personal. Anyone hiring her will be rewarded many times over."

—Joe Christian

Performance Coach

"Betsy is an amazing business woman with dead-on intuition and a plethora of skills and experiences to draw from. I recommend her without reservation."

—Trish Thomas

CEO at Atomic20

"Betsy is a seasoned professional who brings her high energy level and professionalism to everything she does. Having her work with you and your company is a great investment."

—Teena Anderson

Non-Profit Organization Management Professional

Key 5

Exchange

with

Companion Journal

Books By Betsy L. Jordan

Seven Absolute Keys to Create Anything:!

Coach! Seven Keys for the Beginning Coach

Key 1, Oneness, with Companion Journal

Key 2, Inter-Dimension, with Companion Journal

Key 3, Movement, with Companion Journal

Key 4, Paradox, with Companion Journal

Key 5, Exchange, with Companion Journal

Key 6, Personal Power, with Companion Journal

Key 7, Yin/Yang, with Companion Journal

BullsEye!

The Seven Tactics To Hit The Bull's Eye In Your Business

Film Industry Professional's Edition

Book One: Connect!

Book Two: See!

Book Three: Act!

Book Four: Experience!

Book Five: Expand!

Book Six: Power Up!

Book Seven: Launch!

KEY 5

EXCHANGE

WITH

COMPANION JOURNAL

BY BETSY L. JORDAN

Editing, Cover and Book Design by Rodney Miles

Dedicated to my remarkable *mentors.*

They had their work cut out for them!

"The universe rewards expansive plans."

—Julia Cameron

"... and abundant exchange!"

—Betsy Jordan

CONTENTS

AUTHOR'S NOTE

Many coaches will understand the principles covered herein automatically. My desire is that coaches use these universal principles of creativity and develop a language to use in their practices, troubleshooting as they go along. For example, the client who understands "oneness" and networks easily, may need work in the area of "personal power" if they are networking for approval. Or, a client who has no trouble imagining their future (inter-dimension) who yet won't get up off of the sofa needs work in the area of "movement." Let the seven keys be your framework.

Betsy Jordan

EXCHANGE, THE FIFTH KEY

"Our heritage and ideals, our code and standards - the things we live by and teach our children—are preserved or diminished by how freely we exchange ideas and feelings."

—Walt Disney

Introduction

The Difference

How many relationships, jobs, classes, experiences, great ideas, and coaching clients—even, have you experienced in your life? If we are alike in any way, you and I, it's probably safe to assume that we have both had great experiences and achievements, and have both had our share of failures and mishaps, too. In fact there is a lot that ten different jobs, three different careers, moving around the United States, one child, two stepsons, and two marriages will teach you, but the real difference came when I made a few simple changes in my life:

Focus and application.

As a positive, interested human being, I read, watched, listened, attended, and really did absorb a great deal of good information. Still, failure and success seemed somehow determined unconsciously and haphazardly until I focused on what were emerging as key principals and made very sure I applied what seemed true enough to possibly be universal. *Keys* started to rise to the top of my experiences when I employed attentive focus with application. Thrilling—simply thrilling. And today I get to share what I have learned with you, because my life after that point of discovery has been different, to say the least.

Seven *keys* unlock those doors you might have fought to get to, only to find them locked—the few keys that open to your own treasure trove of manifested dreams. These are the few really important doors in life, doors that lead to your own creativity and ability. What others call "luck" is explained in these pages.

But you've heard that before, right? In fact the bookstores are full of books making that very same claim, so what's the difference? Why read this book and others in my series? Simple. *You.* Let's be honest, there is a glut of information—good information—out there and probably even in your own library or on your own Kindle, so why read more? Well, the fact that you *are* reading more tells me two things: for all the good advice you've already found you want more which means you likely have *still* not completely found the right answers for *you*, and second, I believe most advisors do not allow into their equations the most important variable, which is, as I've said, *you.*

I want you to take the Seven Keys and make them yours, to understand these Seven Keys and apply them in *your own* way and to your unique situations and relationships. I want you to find these keys so natural after a period of focus and application that they become second nature, and what others see as a "knack" or "luck" seem to follow you wherever you go. I want you to have your own Midas touch as a result of your new acquaintance with *the Seven Keys.*

And there are seven. Some say this is the number of the mystic and indeed, throughout the ages seven has had a special place in the world. God created the heavens and the Earth in seven days. The Greek God Hermes is credited with scribing an ancient text with seven natural laws. Life itself is often described as having a seven-year cycle (or a seven-year itch). And after all of my own research and observation, the number seven simply seems to present itself universally, and in profound and powerful ways. So, seven it is.

And I now know there is *power* and an ability to *consciously create* what I really want, what you really want. Things are different now, thanks to that *knowledge.* And it did transition from a *belief* to a *knowledge* after consistently getting results with the seven keys. And when I consider sharing this knowledge it strikes me that I have plenty in my own life I wish I had *not* created, but to shy away from these things, you'll see, only pulls us back into the trap that beleaguers most people, the belief that we *cannot* create our own thoughts, that we cannot manifest our own beauty and even our own greatness. In fact, even today when I end up with something that I am not consciously creating, I know that I get to learn from it, but I also know I get to move on from there to consciously change my own thoughts in order to create something different, something desirable. I know that there is power and the ability to consciously create what I really want, when I am fully accountable for it all.

You choose: which is more empowering, when you blame circumstances or people around you for anything non-ideal in your life *or* knowing that you are responsible for all of your life *and can therefore change it*? Important choice to make. And your life is happening *now and you are in it*—this is not a "waiting room" by any means. Too many valuable people still see it that way.

In fact the former choice is actually the more practical one, and before you take any knowledge and consider it, it should, after all, be practical. All my roads have led me here. I have studied with various people, as mentioned I've read, listened, watched, attended, and I've experimented with my own life. I have things in my own background you would be very able to relate to: failures and successes. There are enough of the first that would make us empathetic friends, and plenty of the second that would establish my credibility to lead on this issue, to capture your imagination for self- and world-improvement, just as the discovery of these seven keys has captured mine.

Anyone can learn these seven keys, either for oneself or as a philosophy with which to help others. We all create our worlds subconsciously everyday anyway, why not take charge of that facility? This book is an attempt to give you the tools that I now apply in my own life and my own practice, and these tools can now be shortcuts for you and your own clients!

But it's not magic, either. Learning to be aware takes practice.

Although some very important parts of the process cannot be "seen," they are as real as those parts that you can see. In fact, the world of the "unseen" is arguably more important than the world of the "seen," and this will become more clear as we move forward. With each key that we explain you (and your clients) will be given a chance to work with it, to do exercises which give you a practical experience of the key. I have found—through my own experience and through information that frankly, has simply come through me—that each key has a corresponding chakra, or area in the energetic body to which it corresponds. The chakra system is an energetic system which is explained through Vedic science, and which the Hindu religion has located just outside of the body but close to very specific areas of connection. You can use these areas of the body as touch points to remember the Seven Keys. Other than that, please see the appendix on the chakras at the back of this book and visit texts on the chakra system to understand more about that connection. My intention here is to keep things simple.

The way that I believe creativity comes through most quickly is from the 7th chakra down. In other words, I believe creativity can best be explained from the spiritual plane through manifestation, from the intellectual to the material, and from head to toe. You have a thought, the thought becomes manifest after action is taken.

Yet you do not have to believe this to benefit from the exercises or the information. My intention is to give you the tools to build a foundation for creating the life you dream of, with confidence that you are in tune with the natural elements of the universe, and to do so as quickly as possible.

I wish you all you have ever dreamed of.

And once you've assembled your own *Seven Keys* with focus and application, how will your life be different? How will your coaching practice change? And who will you help?

"I think that connection with humans is so important. Sometimes I'll do this monologue and talk to the crowd, like, 'Come on, let's really connect here.' I don't think a lot of people understand it's a two-way exchange. Some people go to a show and are like, 'Yeah, you make me feel.' That's not how it works."

—Chet Faker

EXCHANGE

The fifth key, the key of exchange, is my next-to-favorite key, the key of responsibility. When you or I say that we gave our power away, that's not really true, now is it? We always own our power. Whether we choose to use it is another story. When we choose not to we're generally a victim of something—a victim of circumstances, a victim of our neighbor, a victim of our moods.

So there is a whole lot that goes into this particular key that I use often in my work because when someone is coming for coaching with me they talk about how they don't like their job, or they don't like this, or they want to move ahead with this or that. When we limit ourselves by not owning our power, when we're not stepping up to being powerful in the world, what we do is we actually sell out on ourselves and we sell out on the people that matter to us in our lives whether it's at work or at home.

The most powerful place in the world to stand or to be or to hold yourself as, is to be the source of everything, to see all of your life as if it is this wonderful classroom type place for you to learn from everywhere, from your relationships, from every interaction you have, even with your computer. And in that place of relationship, if you see yourself as the source of everything then you are able to respond to anything that occurs in a manner that has you being aware of your interpretations.

Notice I said, "being able to respond" instead of saying "be responsible to." When we are responsible for something and we say, "Oh, look at me! I was responsible for that," or when we take credit for something that's really a victim to somebody else's opinion of us. When we see ourselves as being able to respond to anything that occurs, we're able to be flexible. We're able to have our sense of humor about life. We're able to play, as you will. So the most powerful place is to stand in your ability to respond to anything that occurs. In that responsibility, and considering yourself the source of it all, you're standing as someone who is in action in your life, who is in charge of your life.

We, as human beings always have interpretations, assessments, and judgments on everything. We take those interpretations and sometimes turn them into what we believe are facts, but they are not always facts, they are literally interpretations of life. We can become a victim to our interpretations which then has us in a place of less than powerful. So when someone comes in and they're complaining about something, or they are explaining something in a defensive manner, I know that they could be more powerful in the world if they could simply be powerful. And they could come in and say, "Okay, this is what I wish to do with my life."

So you know, when the key of personal power is off kilter, when you are explaining or complaining or justifying, or saying that this person is so and so and coming off with your interpretations as if they are facts, this is the segment that I wish all of America could see. because we are victim to our computers, we're a victim to the internet, we're a victim to a whole bunch of other social ills, we're a victim of the school system, we're a victim of the church—we have a victim mentality. Homeless people, for example, we treat them as though they are victims. We always have a choice in the moment, every single one of us has a choice. So in a place of choosing, of being the ultimate choice maker in your life, you come into the world in a powerful, powerful place. Does a baby not cry when they want attention? And they get it.

They don't sit back and wait for somebody to cry for them. That's a powerful place.

So speak up for what you want. Declare what it is you are going to do and do it, take action toward it. You'll be acting from a place of personal power. How does this fit with creating something new in your life, creating a business or anything else? Well, if it's raining outside you still are creating your business. If something comes up and it seems to be something you did not plan on, had no way of anticipating—or even if you did anticipate it—your place of power is how you react to those things. How do you choose to react to it? Do I choose to interpret it negatively and it sidetracks me, or do I choose to learn from it and then move me forward?

Here's to your being powerful today, and every day of your life. You'll be glad you did.

"If my love is without sacrifice, it is selfish. Such a love is barter, for there is exchange of love and devotion in return for something. It is conditional love."

—Sadhu Vaswani

OUT FROM UNDER THE INFLUENCE

With my clients, I am often coaching about ways of being responsible or accountable so that they remain in the driver's seat of their lives, especially when I hear statements like "I can't afford it," or "I don't have time," "Business is horrible," or "In this economy, I can't," or "That's good—for this economy," or "I need to lose weight."

It's a fact, if you look at current externals such as economic indicators, the Weather Channel, Fox News, the DOW, we should all hide our money under our mattresses, pull our covers over our heads and not come out again for a few years. I, for one, choose to see things differently.

I have all that I need in this moment.

Think about that. Say it out loud. In this present moment, you are breathing, your heart is beating, you literally have everything that you need to survive. Once you own that thought turn your focus inward. Think about what you want to have, in addition to having what you need. Then take a deep, expansive breath and close your eyes.

Imagine that you have all that you desire, that this special moment somehow is transformed to the moment after having it all. What is that for you? And now, how are you feeling? Generally, the world is a happier place, once you move from external influences, to internal referral. At the very least, you will feel less anxious, more in control of your world. And from that happier place, make decisions that will move you forward, out from under the influence of what *they* are saying out there!

"Love consists in giving without getting in return; in giving what is not owed, what is not due the other. That's why true love is never based, as associations for utility or pleasure are, on a fair exchange."

—Mortimer Adler

Turn the Page

Have you ever had a conversation with a friend where you were sharing good news and they reminded you to be cautious? Does a parent ever "remind" you of the time you did "thus and so" as a warning, of course, not to get too excited! Have your well-meaning relatives "reminded" you that you have a past with them, and that they don't agree with your new ideas?

Argue for your limitations and you will surely keep them. In other words, turn off the voices. Request that you be allowed to grow and change in your relationships, request that others release your "history." Look forward.

When you argue for your limitations, or for the limitations of others, you create and focus on doubt. When you focus on doubt; doubt grows. When you focus on success, success grows. Try it.

Once you risk letting your relatives see you differently. (And they *will,* when you let them know that their "reminders" bother you.), your request of them to not "hold you in your history" then requires *you* to do the same for them. It may amuse you that the issue then becomes about you allowing *them* to change enough to honor your request.

Turn the page.

"The most important single central fact about a free market is that no exchange takes place unless both parties benefit."

—Milton Friedman

DEAR COACHES

The key of exchange is all about exchanging negative for positive energy. Truly when you inspire your clients to be accountable for their energy, for their thoughts, for their actions, for their words, you are exercising the principle of exchange. It's not a secret that when people are afraid they withdraw. They draw in; their countenance even gets pinched. And when someone is brave and joyously sharing their bravery, they are open, showing up bigger. Their face is broader because they're not pinched. We're looking at inspiring our clients, mentoring them, coaching them into being open, and broader, in their thinking and their actions.

It's not enough just to have a dream and then intention. It's important to also share the dream and intention to create team in the world. Nothing is ever accomplished alone.

"I'm very happy to hear that my work inspires writers and painters. It's the most beautiful compliment, the greatest reward. Art should always be an exchange."

—Nick Cave

GIVING AND RECEIVING

So many of us have heard about the power of giving. And there is power in giving and receiving. Yet there is a subtler way of looking at giving. It matters whether you give from "having something" or from not "having something," from "wanting something," from not "wanting something."

The exercises in this book will support this.

"I always try to teach by example and not force my ideas on a young musician. One of the reasons we're here is to be a part of this process of exchange."

—Dizzy Gillespie

CONCLUSION

The Seven Keys are here for you, unearthed and available to you. I can show and describe them but only you can pick them up and approach your goals and dreams with them, ready to unlock the barriers so many others find impassable. It's my hope that you *try* them after understanding them, that you perfect their use, that you use this and all books on the subject to improve first your own life and then the lives of your clients. I hope they become second nature to you. All of us can benefit massively from a knowledge of the Seven Keys and if we coach others they become even more important, so that we and our clients can create what we want, right where we are. We no longer need to wonder, be frustrated, or seek the approval of others or even the environment.

Armed with this book series you can make a difference. These books are not the fastest route, however, to learning the Seven Keys and their application. That comes from a live event, where through your own commitment and focus, your results will be fast and powerful. See the back of this book to discover how you can attend a seminar or webinar, how you can become certified in the training of others in The Seven Keys, and how you too can benefit from receiving coaching as well as from delivering it. It might be easier than you think to get connected, but even were it not, what would it be worth to train in tapping into your own massive creativity? What about your clients?

And never think that seeking improvement suggests you lack in any way. You have all you need right now, right where you are. The trick is getting to it. We are each whole and complete beings, with untapped potential and an opportunity for actualization. We can each make our dreams come true. Holding a client, friend, or loved one to a higher standard is also not to make less of someone, but more, especially if they themselves desire it. Many don't seem to desire it simply because they are unaware or do not believe it's possible. We know better.

You are uniquely you, and the only one. And you are complete. You only need to unlock what lies inside.

I hope that you take these keys and unlocking your barriers, live the life I believe you deserve. I hope you find abundance in all you seek in whatever arenas you find you love, and in whatever form this may be. I hope you find this all to be an incredible adventure, because it is just that—the adventure of *you.* And you have gifts for the world, that the world needs and needs badly.

Give a man a fish and he eats for perhaps a day, but teach him to fish and he can feed himself, his family, his friends and community as long as there are fish. And when we create abundance for those around us we seem to have it ourselves. When we see strength, intelligence, goodness in others and grant them as much we have effectively created those things or at least planted the seeds of those things. The opposite is, well, the opposite. *Pity,* for example. When given or received leads to weakness and a weakened relationship as well. Any immediate gratification is short lived, of course. In fact taken to an extreme, this is the road to resentment! Giving when you lack leads only to more lack if you are giving only with the intention of feeling better or bigger yourself. Giving from a place of abundance however, creates it for everyone.

Giving with the idea of improving someone else's life *while also* improving your own is about one of life's greatest answers. The greatest partnerships—whether it's a husband and wife, business partners, or even a coach and client—are created by two wholly independent people who choose to be together because they can and want to be together. Partnerships created out of dependency leave one partner stronger than the other. They spiral downward as they are based on contraction, lack, and fear.

Yet we are, each of us, whole and complete beings.

And there is nothing broken about you or your clients, only untapped, locked away, in ways unique to each client. In fact we only do maintenance and development here, the repair shop is somewhere else. And part of that development is first recognizing, which is easy to do, the magnificence in each person. All you need to do is look.

May you celebrate your magnificence and that of each client through a life of passionate work and sound knowledge, may you and those you help then bring your own special gifts to the world!

Grounded in the Key of Oneness,

Understanding the influence of the Key of Inter-Dimension,

Executing the Key of Movement,

Choosing in the Key of Paradox,

And sharing in the Key of Exchange,

That which you want the most, brings more of what you want quickly into your life!

"When a positive exchange between a brand and customers becomes quantifiable metrics, it encourages brand to provide better service, customer service to do a better job, and consumers to actively show their gratitude."

—Simon Mainwaring

THE 7 KEYS

TO CREATING THE LIFE YOU HAVE DREAMED OF!

Key #1, Oneness

Key #2, Inter-Dimension

Key #3, Movement

Key #4, Paradox

Key #5, Exchange

Key #6, Personal Power

Key #7, Yin~Yang

COMPANION JOURNAL

"Live interaction with a crowd is a cathartic, spiritual kind of exchange, and it's intensified at a festival."

—Trent Reznor

Exercise ~ Childhood and Money

1. Think about your childhood. Write about two events where you did something with money or had an experience with someone else about money.

2. Notice what was said or done about money.

3. As an adult, how does your conversation about money echo your earliest experiences?

4. Notice if you make your money decisions from an expansive or contracted place.

Exercise ~ Distance

1. Think about your relationships with people. Are you speaking first? Are you waiting for someone else to break the ice?

2. What do you do when you sense that someone is distant? Notice what is happening in your gut.

3. Are you reacting with an expansive thought or a contracted one?

Exercise ~ Three Ways

1. Write three ways to improve your relationships at home and at work by noticing the key of exchange.

2. Write three ways to improve your financial condition by noticing the key of exchange.

Exercise ~ Place Your Thought

1. Find a partner and sit in front of them.

2. Place your thoughts on what you would like to create, on your vision for your life.

3. Choose who goes first.

4. The person who goes first starts talking about their vision. The listening partner asks questions and evokes abundance and accountability. Make sure you break through limitations.

5. Evoke a larger vision with them. Be in their vision as if you were creating it. Make it bigger. Expand it. Come from abundance.

6. Notice different ways to expand it, to go deeper. Go broader.

7. Switch partners so now the second partner talks about their vision. Again the listening partner finds ways to expand it, to go deeper and broader.

8. Imagine that you have zero limits, go where you didn't think you could go. Go where you stretch.

9. Discuss with your partner what this exchange meant for you.

Exercise ~ One Million Dollars

PART ONE

Take a check out of your check book and write it out for *one million dollars* ($1,000,000.00), made out to you and date it a year from now. Imagine that you have one million dollars in your bank account. This is an ongoing exercise.

Take 365 days and divide the million dollars equally over those days, and every day “spend” (in your mind) $2,739. There will be days when you forget to spend it. Now you're not really spending this money, you are virtually spending this money. You're not online purchasing either. What you are doing is getting in the habit of what you would spend your money on if you had it.

So chances are if you find a deal on something that you really and truly want, you are going to visualize having it. The habit you get into is “I'm gonna spend $2,739 virtually today, and I'm going to buy this and this and this,” and when you're buying it all you're doing so freely, you're purchasing that feeling in your mind.

Some days when you forget to spend your money you will add the set amount from the day before to your purchase today. Write all of these down. Write every day’s exercise and your balance down in a calendar. At the end of every week go back and visualize having those things that you pseudo-purchased. You will know your answer to the question "If you had one million dollars, what would you spend it on?

What would you use it for?

We know that a million dollars doesn't go quite as far as it used to go. We also know that in some countries a million dollars is a great deal of money.

We want you to be in the habit of focusing on what you *can* have instead of what you cannot.

Get in the habit of an abundance mentality.

When you're spending your million dollars you are creating wealth for other people. There will be very few ways you could spend the million dollars and not affect others. It's about *abundant exchange*, and in building that for other people you will see that.

Some of you are familiar with the law of attraction—this is pretty much like that, however we are not asking you to take specific action by going out and spending your money or by tithing in the collection plate by going and giving money away, money which you do not have. People who have abundant wealth generally know exactly where they wanted to go and why.

Money is important to people living in abundant wealth consciousness. They declared it to be so, and so it is. Money is only one way of looking at abundance. So look at the things that you do spend your money on in this exercise.

PART TWO

A second part of this exercise is to write what you actually *did* spend your money on. Write everything down. Keep your receipts and look at those credit card statements. Make a list every day of what you spent that day. You will find that there are places where you can create additional abundance in your life.

Change your habits. Take a look at those places where you're spending extra money and save it instead. Put it in a jar and decide what you're going to spend it on that would have you feeling abundant.

After the second month you should know where you are going to save money.

Decide how you're going to allocate that money. It is amazing how much we can end up with if we just pay attention.

If you do not have a lot of money in your bank account then it's important not to give it away because you then create more *lack* in your life. What you want to do is to give from a place of abundance, but really give to a purpose.

Exercise ~ Unlocking with The Keys

The key of oneness explains the idea that if we are arguing with someone in this part of the world, this leaves a mark on someone else in another place. It's not a chain reaction or anything as clearly direct, yet it has an effect just the same. It explains why Mother Teresa would say, "You will not see me at an anti-war rally. If you have a peace rally, please invite me." She understood oneness, as well as polarity or paradox and expansion versus contraction. She knew we are all connected, she knew to focus on the thing that is the highest and best good to get the results she wanted, and she also knew that what she placed her attention on would expand.

All of the keys overlap. The process of creativity is integrated and happens regardless of what we think about it. We are always breathing, our blood is always pumping. We create new cells in our body every second. With every thought that we think; we are creating. At the level of thought and emotion, we can affect things in the world that we do not see.

In the following exercise, when we tested it, we found that it was effective in demonstrating that we can affect others simply by our thoughts and feelings. I was surprised when we discovered that the person with their eyes closed would often respond or react and not even be aware of their reactions! I see this exercise now as a way to illustrate the key of exchange, the key of oneness, the key of inter-dimension, the key of paradox, the key of personal power on a subtle level. However, I believe it applies best to the key of movement as it clearly shows we affect others by our own thoughts, and that once we accept that we do, we can affect everything around us by never even saying a word.

1. Put one person in the front of the room with their eyes closed or blindfolded.

2. You or someone else act as facilitator, and you whisper to other participants a word such as joy, sexiness, frustration, etc.

3. The participants go up one by one and without saying a word, they do their best to generate the word that they are given in the person who has their eyes closed.

4. After a short while ask the person at the front of the room to open his or her eyes or remove the blindfold, and talk about their thoughts during the exercise.

"We believe that business is good because it creates value. It is ethical because it is based on voluntary exchange; it is noble because it can elevate our existence, and it is heroic because it lifts people out of poverty and creates prosperity."

—John Mackey

ABOUT BETSY JORDAN

Betsy Jordan holds a PhD in Experiential Training through the Legacy Center, and Direct Impact. Further training in leadership development and coaching helped her focus on how we can effectively cause transformation in our lives and businesses. "The river that runs through my career is the exciting world of human development." She has studied with Deepak Chopra, MD., becoming one of the first mind/body educators in the country. "Studying with Deepak helped me to see the science behind thoughts causing reactions in our bodies". That degree opened doors for her work in quality customer service with major corporations in hospital supplies and banking industries. Betsy has a BS in Business Administration from the University of North Carolina at Chapel Hill.

Betsy's life experiences have encompasses the creative community, the corporate world and the unique challenges of entrepreneurship. Whatever challenges you face, she is the coach who can relate, resolve problems, and turbo-charge your results. Her pioneering work on creativity is published in her book, *Seven Absolute Keys to Create Anything!* as well as a number of forthcoming publications. Please watch for new titles and materials as they are released.

START TODAY!

THE TIME TO BEGIN your perfecting of the seven keys is *right now.* Your full life of passion, your independence from waiting on politicians to gain their senses or the film industry to seek you out is at hand.

www.BullsEyeCoach.com

SEMINARS & WEBINARS

FIND OUT ABOUT UPCOMING seminars and webinars by visiting this website:

www.BullsEyeCoach.com

COACHING

AND FOR YOUR QUICKEST route to perfecting the seven tactics and to experience The BullsEyeCoaching™ process (which includes the seven tactics), *contact me today.* I look forward to meeting you and hearing your ideas!

info@BullsEyeCoach.com

ACKNOWLEDGEMENTS

THIS IS A WORK about life. I could say that I thank everyone who ever touched my life directly and indirectly for all of you have been teachers, and I mean that sincerely. In this way, you all have contributed to the writing of this book.

To my mentors, all of you: Ray, Michael, Lori, Rob, James, Sam. Let me leave a special notice to my mentor, Deepak Chopra, whose groundbreaking work in the psycho-physiological origins of disease taught me so much about how the mind and the body are related. Through Carolyn Myss in her *Anatomy of the Spirit* I recognize that even in irreverence there is still reverence.

Thanks to Louise Hay whose bravery and generosity has helped so many people overcome ailments in the body. To my mentors at the legacy center, Robb and Lori in particular, I thank you so much for the true stand you are in the world for so many people. For my mentor Michael Strasner who sees the humor in all things and always finds that balance.

To my former husbands both of whom taught me the extraordinary strength and power of faith. To the great loves of my life who are numerous and so I would rather they know who they are and be grateful that we had that love. Once I choose to love someone, I *always* do, even if we disagree.

Sean Roach, I wouldn't have ever thought about writing these books if not for your brilliance and direction. And Rodney Miles, thank you so much for your contribution above expectations and execution of this series. I look forward to many, many years with this team of amazing people.

To the boys of my heart, Kyle and Taylor, who taught me that parenting had nothing to do with being of the same genetic make-up. And finally, to my sensitive and brilliant daughter who shows me every day what a miracle life is.

THE CHAKRAS

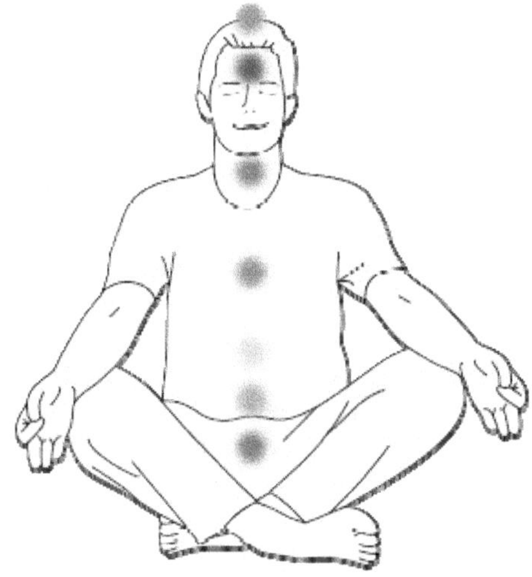

Figure 1: The seven chakras and their locations in the body.

The word "chakra" comes from a Sanskrit word meaning "wheel," (or "spinning point of light) and in some religions of India are considered points of energy and part of the intangible body that influences the physical body. Energy channels through these points. While there are believed to be many and various *nodes* or chakras throughout our bodies, these are the seven most important.

According to Caroline Myss in her book *Anatomy of the Spirit,* all of our thoughts and experiences are filtered through these chakras which function in part as databases, and are associated with our physical and mental selves as well as certain colors.

Some associate the chakras with specific nerve centers and glandular functions, and each is associated with various energies, all of which can be understood and placed into harmony.

THE 7 KEYS

TO CREATING THE LIFE YOU HAVE DREAMED OF!

Key #1, Oneness

Key #2, Inter-Dimension

Key #3, Movement

Key #4, Paradox

Key #5, Exchange

Key #6, Personal Power

Key #7, Yin~Yang

7 KEYS SUMMARIES

Key 1, Oneness

Oneness, all, we are the same stuff, we affect and are affected by each other, remove judgment of self and others.

Located above the head. 7th Chakra.

Key 2, Inter-Dimension

Inter-dimension, all levels, all of the time, awareness at the level of "before language," thoughts become things, know what you "know."

Located between the eyes (third eye). 6th Chakra.

Key 3, Movement

Movement, constant motion even at subtle levels... everything moving, language is the great creator, in the beginning was the Word, Thumper in the movie *Bambi* was correct: “If you can’t say somethin’ nice, don’t say nothin’ at all.” Even subtler, if you can’t “think “anything nice, then don’t think anything at all, or at the very least, get outta the room!

Located at the throat (voice box). 5th Chakra.

Key 4, Paradox

Paradox, in every challenge lies the seed of its solution. Opposites exist. Polarity. Focus on positive and dismiss all lack and thoughts of lack. Want lots of goodies in your life, warm and fuzzies? Create it for others. Want love? Create it in every interaction. What we focus on expands. Decide with the heart.

Located above the heart. 4th Chakra.

Key 5, Exchange

Exchange, the Universe (God) rewards expansive plans. Giving and receiving both are expansive actions. Taking is a contracting energy—it interrupts expansion and leads to contraction. Give what you most want in a manner that creates this for others. Associated with gut feeling or solar plexus.

Located above the solar plexus. 3rd Chakra.

Key 6, Personal Power

Personal power, we are all whole and complete, no matter what our size and shape, number of fingers and toes, we can never give our power away. In our most complete and powerful understanding of ourselves, we understand the laws of cause and effect. We are able to respond to it all. Owning our power means that we have released "victim" consciousness. From the place of personal strength, ownership of it all, we can create something different. There is nothing more powerful than *you!*

Located above the abdomen. 2nd Chakra.

Key 7, Yin/Yang

Male/female, there lies within us the feminine and masculine principles and properties of creativity. Feminine is nurturing, gestational, conceptual, and spiritual. Masculine is assertive, action-oriented, physical, and material. When in balance, beautiful and powerful creations are born. When out of balance, depression and sometimes even war ensue.

Located at the root or genital area. 1st Chakra.

7 KEYS & THE CHAKRAS

Key #1, Oneness
Located above the head. 7th Chakra.

Key #2, Inter-Dimension
Located between the eyes (third eye). 6th Chakra.

Key #3, Movement
Located at the throat (voice box). 5th Chakra.

Key #4, Paradox
Located above the heart. 4th Chakra.

Key #5, Exchange
Located above the solar plexus. 3rd Chakra.

Key #6, Personal Power
Located above the abdomen. 2nd Chakra.

Key #7, Yin~Yang
Located at the root or genital area. 1st Chakra.

SUCCESS STORIES

The following case studies assure you that the process works! And this format keeps us from sharing confidential information.

THE LESSON

Do it Your Way

A frustrated employee turned budding entrepreneur discovered her true path.

This client came to me knowing that things weren't right at work. She'd known this for awhile. She wanted guidance. In pattern interruption the image she pulled was of her on the beach talking with Jesus. (This image is always the perfect one for you, chosen by you, in the perfect time to answer your intended result.) His words, according to what she saw were, "You go back and do what you need to do. I am with you. I've done this my way, you do it your way." I watched her progress from afar. After this experience, she had the courage to start her business. It is gradually growing—her way. It's a great gift to the world, and a great gift from her heart. The image she held in her mind's eye that day gave her strength, courage and insight to boldly proceed in the direction of her dreams.

THE LESSON

The Power of Saying, "No"

A very powerful educated attorney had a vision, yet didn't know what to do about it.

My trademarked seven-step TurboCoaching program showed us that the step involving personal power was out of balance. Once this client got clear on his vision for his company, he was able to make requests with urgency. This got him an audience with a major U.S. corporate CEO which led to a future relationship with that corporate leader. Two months was all he needed. His life and his work were transformed, and his vision came to life.

THE LESSON

Don't Ignore the Shadow Side

Yet another study involved a public relations professional.

Her life was grounded in involvement with people. She knew her professional life was in good shape; yet her personal relationships would falter. She chose pattern interruption and discovered a subconscious stumbling block. The image in her subconscious was of her dad. During the session she pulled an image showing that she adored him, and then, she saw a dark side that she had never consciously acknowledged. Through the interpretation session she was able to see that she denied the shadow side in any of her relationships. Once she was aware of this pattern of denial, she was able to create relationships with people which were authentic, embracing both the lighter and darker sides of their personalities. When those sides were extreme, she could walk away without harm.

www.ingramcontent.com/pod-product-compliance
Lightning Source LLC
Chambersburg PA
CBHW071819200526
45169CB00018B/447

* 9 7 8 1 5 2 3 8 2 8 4 4 9 *